UKULELE
MISTER ROGERS SONGBOOK

2   Are You Brave?

3   Days of the Week

4   Everything Grows Toge[...]

5   Going to Marry Mom

6   Happy Birthday, Happy

8   I Like to Be Told

7   I'm Taking Care of You

10   It's Such a Good Feeling

12   It's You I Like

14   Just for Once

16   Let's Think of Something to Do (While We're Waiting)

18   One and One Are Two

19   Peace and Quiet

20   Please Don't Think It's Funny

22   Sometimes

26   Sometimes People Are Good

28   There Are Many Ways (To Say I Love You)

23   What Do You Do?

40   When a Baby Comes

30   When the Day Turns to Night

32   Won't You Be My Neighbor?
(It's a Beautiful Day in the Neighborhood)

34   You Can Never Go Down the Drain

36   You're Growing

38   You've Got to Do It

ISBN 978-1-5400-4351-1

Visit Hal Leonard Online at
www.halleonard.com

Contact us:
Hal Leonard
7777 West Bluemound Road
Milwaukee, WI 53213
Email: info@halleonard.com

In Europe, contact:
Hal Leonard Europe Limited
42 Wigmore Street
Marylebone, London, W1U 2RN
Email: info@halleonardeurope.com

In Australia, contact:
Hal Leonard Australia Pty. Ltd.
4 Lentara Court
Cheltenham, Victoria, 3192 Australia
Email: info@halleonard.com.au

Are You Brave?

Words and Music by Fred Rogers

Days of the Week

Words and Music by Fred Rogers

Everything Grows Together

Words and Music by Fred Rogers

1.–8. Ev - 'ry - thing grows to - geth - er _____ be - cause you're all one

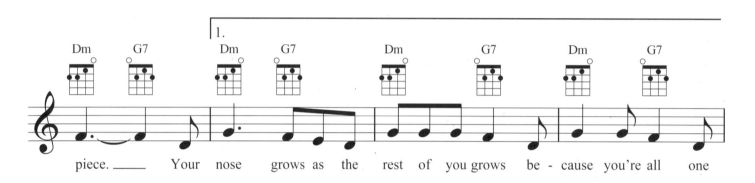

piece. _____ Your nose grows as the rest of you grows be - cause you're all one

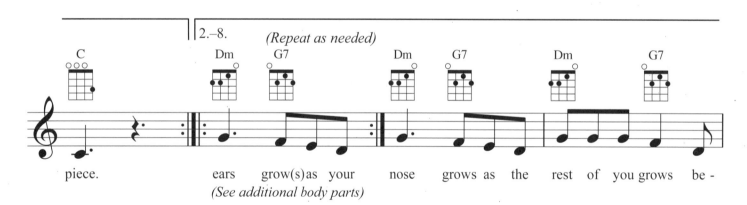

piece. _____ ears grow(s) as your nose grows as the rest of you grows be -
(See additional body parts)

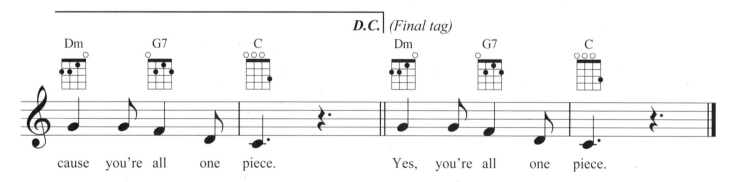

cause you're all one piece. Yes, you're all one piece.

Additional body parts

1. (nose)   5. fingers
2. (ears)   6. legs
3. arms   7. feet
4. hands   8. toes

Going to Marry Mom

Words and Music by Fred Rogers

First note

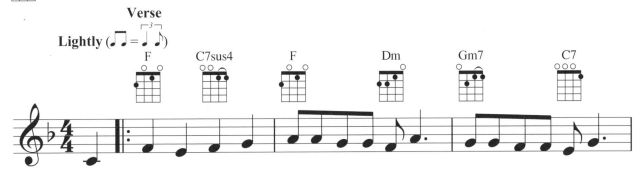

1. One day I said, "I'm real-ly going to mar-ry, real-ly going to mar-ry,
(2.–8.) *See additional lyrics*

real - ly going to mar - ry," I told my mom, "I'm real - ly going to mar - ry,

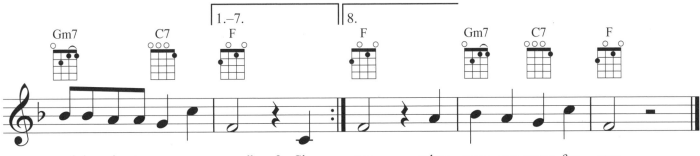

real - ly going to mar - ry you." 2. She ten when some-one cares for you.

Additional Lyrics

2. She smiled, didn't laugh, said,
   "I hope you will marry, I hope you will marry,
   I hope you will marry,"
   She smiled, didn't laugh, said,
   "I hope you will marry,
   Maybe someone like me."

3. "But you see," she said, "I'm *(already married)**…
   I'm married to your daddy."

4. "And as you grow more and *(more like your daddy)**…
   You'll find a person like me."

5. "And she'll love you as *(I love your daddy)**…
   And she will marry you."

6. That's what Mom said when I *(told her I would marry)**… her.

7. I'm glad I told her 'cause I *(really often wondered)**…
   Who my wife would be.

8. It all works out if you *(talk and you listen)**…
   When someone cares for you.

* *Repeat as needed.*

Happy Birthday, Happy Birthday

Words and Music by Fred Rogers

First note

Chorus
Joyfully

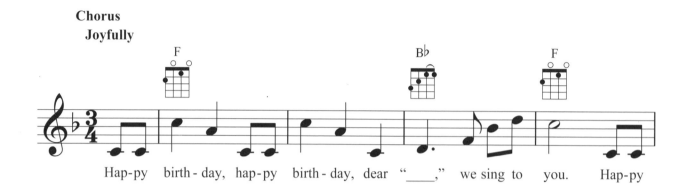

Hap-py birth-day, hap-py birth-day, dear "___," we sing to you. Hap-py

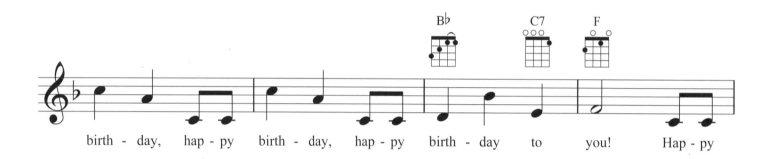

birth - day, hap - py birth - day, hap - py birth - day to you! Hap - py

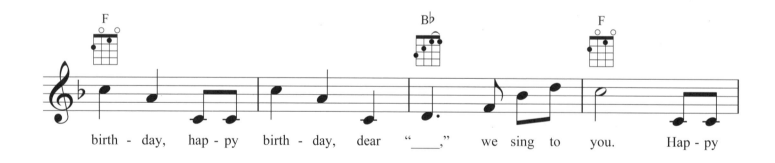

birth - day, hap - py birth - day, dear "___," we sing to you. Hap - py

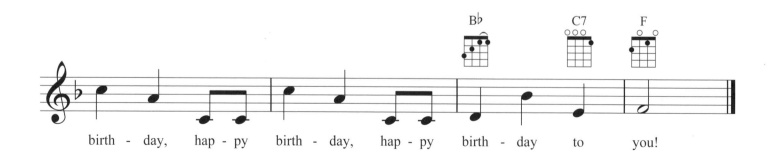

birth - day, hap - py birth - day, hap - py birth - day to you!

I'm Taking Care of You

Words and Music by Fred Rogers

I Like to Be Told

Words and Music by Fred Rogers

trust you more and more   each   time that I'm   find - ing those things to   be

Outro-Verse

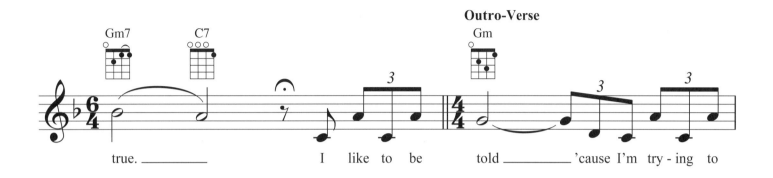

true. _____   I like to be   told _____ 'cause I'm try - ing to

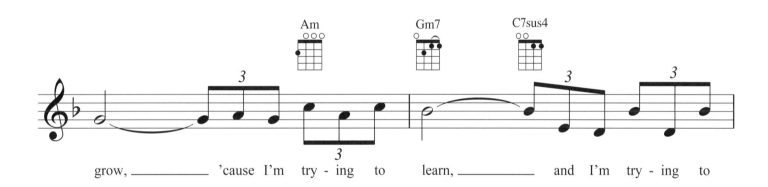

grow, _____ 'cause I'm try - ing to   learn, _____ and I'm try - ing to

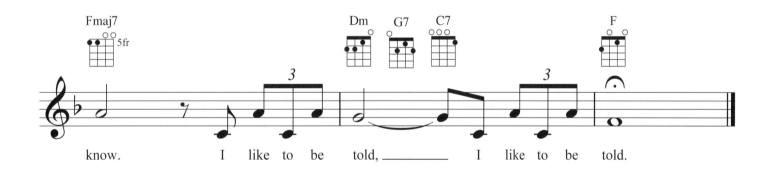

know.   I like to be   told, _____   I like to be told.

Additional Lyrics

2. I like to be told
   If it's going to hurt,
   If it's going to be hard,
   If it's not going to hurt,
   I like to be told,
   I like to be told.

It's Such a Good Feeling

Words and Music by Fred Rogers

First note

Chorus
Moderately bright

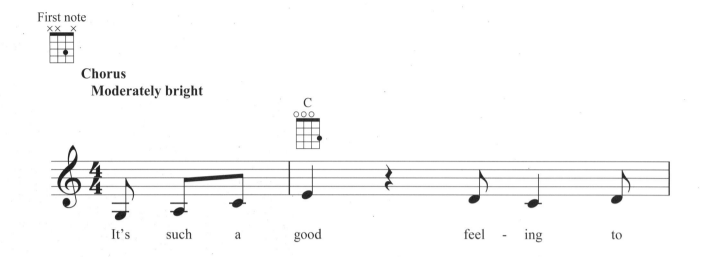

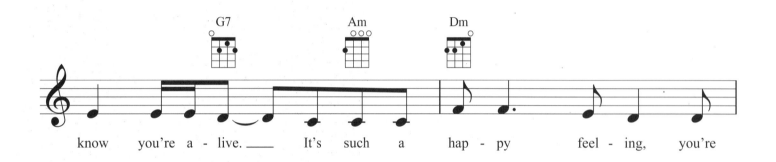

It's such a good feel - ing to

know you're a - live. ___ It's such a hap - py feel - ing, you're

growing in - side. ___ And when you wake up read - y to say, ___

"I think I'll make a snap - py new

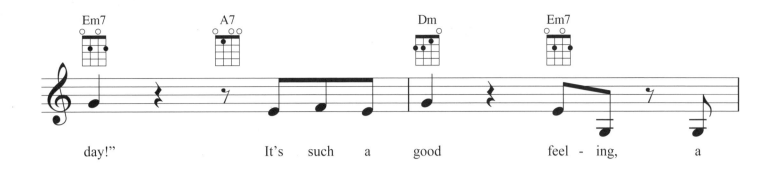

day!"   It's   such   a   good   feel - ing,   a

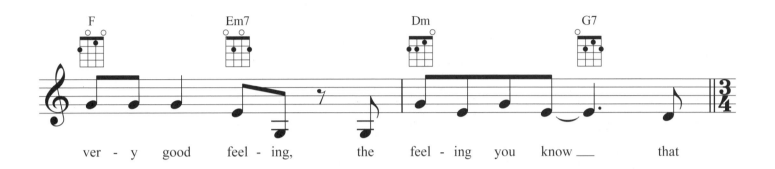

ver - y   good   feel - ing,   the   feel - ing   you   know ___   that

Slower, freely

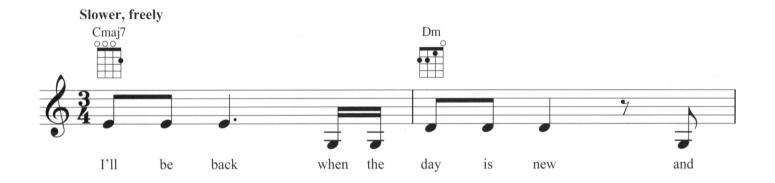

I'll   be   back   when   the   day   is   new   and

I'll   have   more   i - deas   for   you.   And   you'll   have   things   you'll

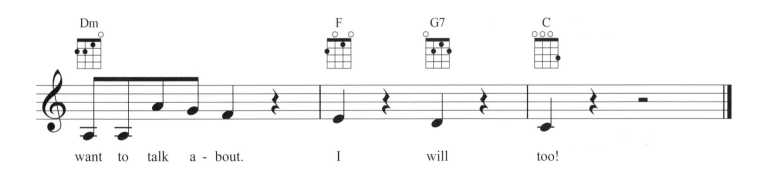

want   to   talk   a - bout.   I   will   too!

It's You I Like

Words and Music by Fred Rogers

like,   ev - 'ry   part   of   you.   Your

skin,   your   eyes,   your   feel - ings,   wheth - er old   or

new.   I   hope   that   you'll   re - mem - ber   e - ven

when you're feel - ing   blue,   that   it's   you   I   like.   It's

you   your - self.   It's   you,   it's

you   I   like.

Just for Once

Words and Music by Fred Rogers

First note

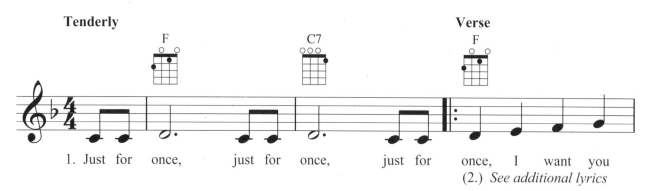

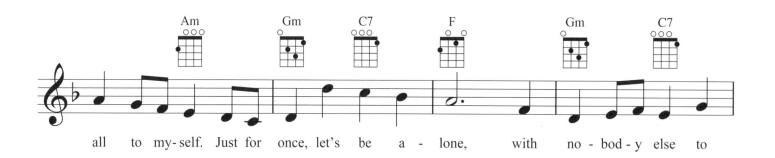

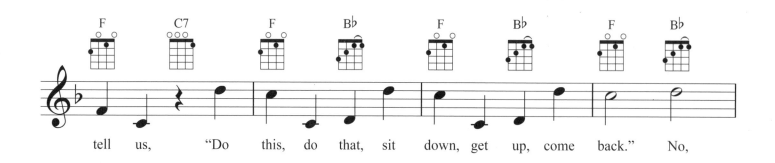

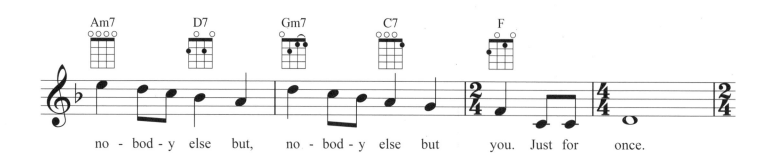

Additional Lyrics

2. Just for once, I want you all to myself.
   Just for once, let's play alone
   With nobody else. We'll build us
   A house with…a garden —
   And no, no, nobody else but,
   Nobody else but you.
   Just for once.

Let's Think of Something to Do
(While We're Waiting)

Words and Music by Fred Rogers

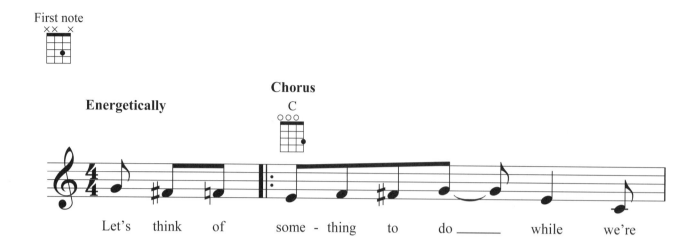

Let's think of some - thing to do ____ while we're

wait - ing, ____ while we're wait - ing ____ for some - thing

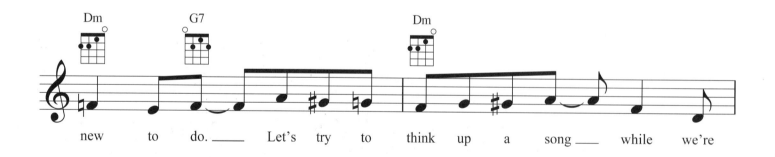

new to do. ____ Let's try to think up a song ____ while we're

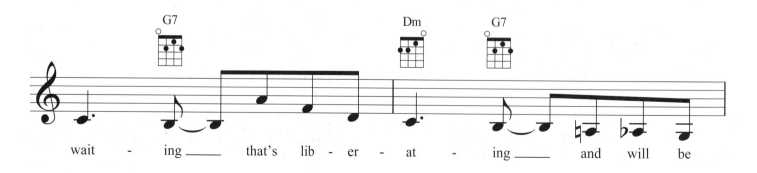

wait - ing ____ that's lib - er - at - ing ____ and will be

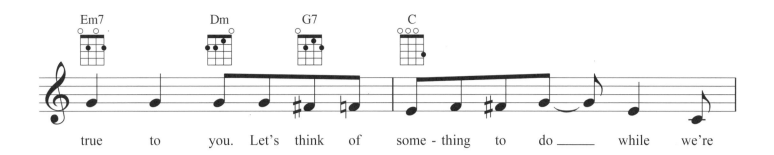

true   to   you.   Let's   think   of   some - thing   to   do _____ while   we're

wait - ing, _____   while   we're   wait - ing _____   'til   some - thing's

through. _____   You   know   it's   real - ly   al - right, ___   in   fact,   it's

down - right   quite   bright ___   to   think   of   some - thing   to   do _____ that's   spe -

cif - ic   for   you. ___   Let's   think   of   some - thing   to   do _____ while   we're

1.
wait - ing.   Let's   think   of

2.
wait - ing.

One and One Are Two

Words and Music by Fred Rogers

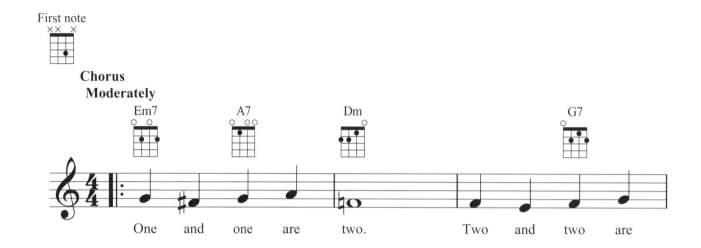

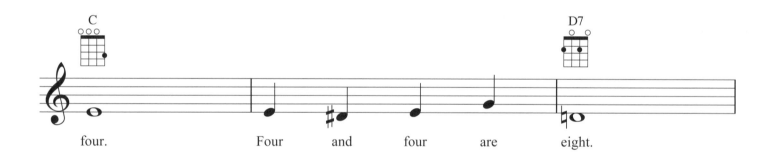

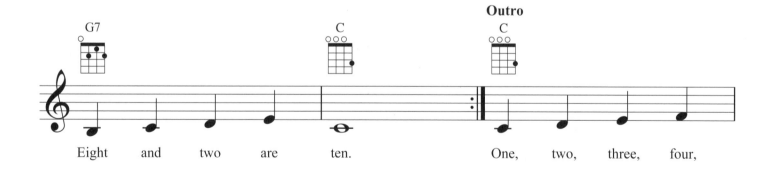

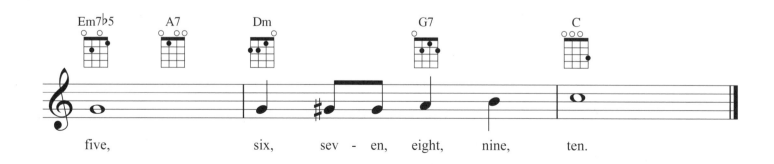

Peace and Quiet

Words and Music by Fred Rogers

First note

Peace and qui - et, peace, peace, peace. Peace and qui - et,

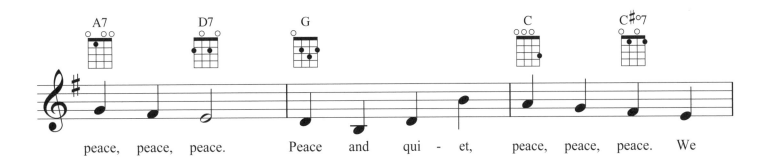

peace, peace, peace. Peace and qui - et, peace, peace, peace. We

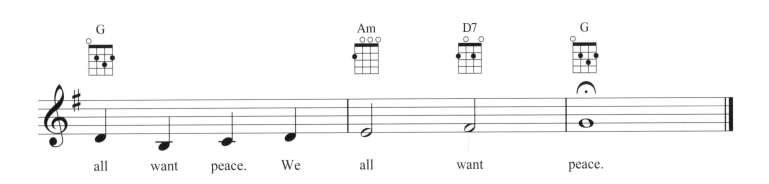

all want peace. We all want peace.

Please Don't Think It's Funny

Words and Music by Fred Rogers

1. Some - times you feel like hold - ing your pil - low all night
(2., 3.) *See additional lyrics*

long. _____ Some - times you hug your ted - dy bear tight - ly; he's old, but he's still

strong. _____ And some-times you want to snug - gle up close - ly with your own mom or

dad. _____ At night you e - ven need the light, some - times, but that's not

Additional Lyrics

2. It's great to know you're growing up
   Bigger every day.
   But somehow things you like to remember
   Are often put away.
   And sometimes you wonder over and over
   If you should stay inside.
   When you enjoy a younger toy…
   You never need to hide.

3. In the long, long trip of growing
   There are stops along the way
   For thoughts of all the soft things
   And a look at yesterday.
   For a chance to fill our feelings,
   With comfort and with ease,
   And then tell the new tomorrow,
   "You can come now when you please."

Sometimes

Words and Music by Fred Rogers

First note

Verse
Moderately

1. Some-times   I   don't feel   like   comb - ing   my   hair.   I
2.–4. *See additional lyrics*

don't feel   like   wash - ing   my   face   some- times.   Some-times   I

don't feel   like   say - ing   "o - kay,"   but   some - times

1.–3.   4.

is - n't   al - ways.   al - ways. _____

Additional Lyrics

2. Sometimes I do feel like combing my hair.
   I do feel like washing my face sometimes.
   Sometimes I do feel like saying "okay,"
   But sometimes isn't always.

3. Sometimes I don't feel like going to bed.
   I don't feel like getting right up sometimes.
   Sometimes I don't feel like wearing my shoes,
   But sometimes isn't always.

4. Sometimes I don't feel like sometimes I do.
   I feel like I don't like to feel sometimes.
   Sometimes I don't and sometimes I do,
   But sometimes isn't always.

What Do You Do?

Words and Music by Fred Rogers

First note

Chorus
With a bounce

What do you do ___ with the mad that you feel ___ when you

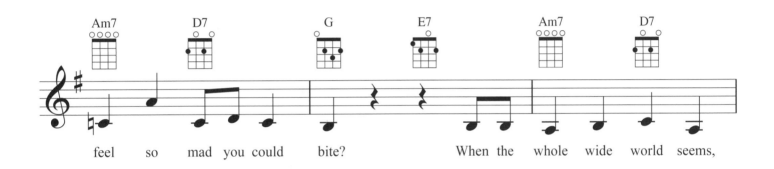

feel so mad you could bite? When the whole wide world seems,

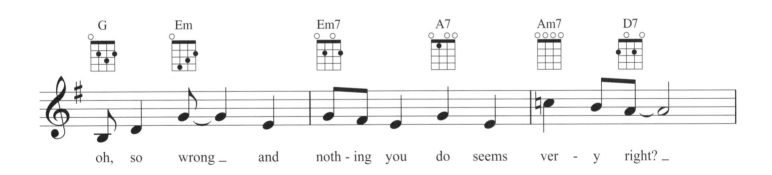

oh, so wrong ___ and noth-ing you do seems ver - y right? ___

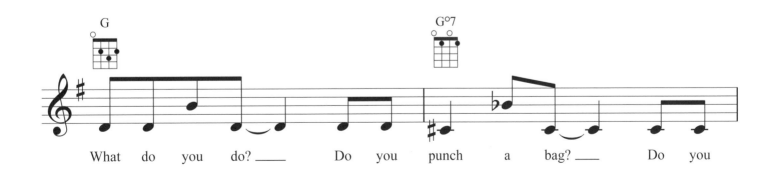

What do you do? ___ Do you punch a bag? ___ Do you

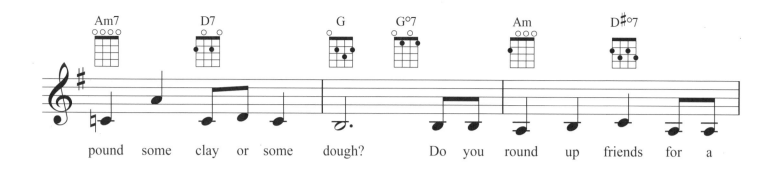

pound   some   clay   or   some   dough?   Do   you   round   up   friends   for   a

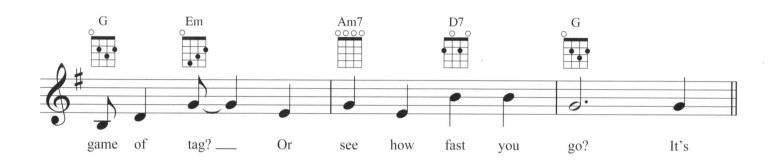

game   of   tag? ___   Or   see   how   fast   you   go?   It's

Bridge
Slower, freely

great   to   be   a - ble   to   stop   when you've planned   a   thing that's   wrong. ___   And   be

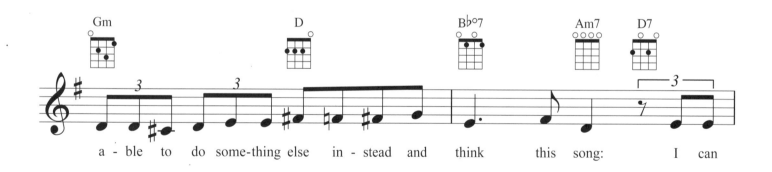

a - ble   to   do   some-thing else   in - stead   and   think   this   song: I   can

Tempo I

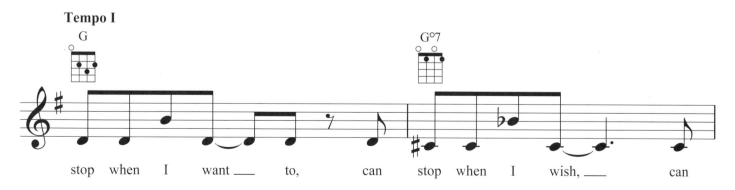

stop   when   I   want ___   to,   can   stop   when   I   wish, ___   can

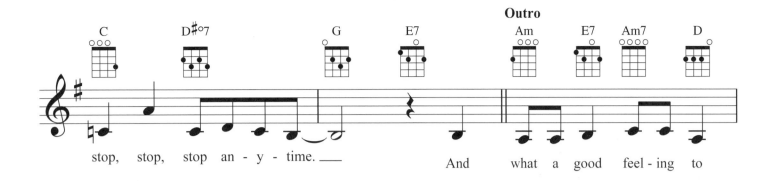

Outro

stop, stop, stop an - y - time. ___ And what a good feel - ing to

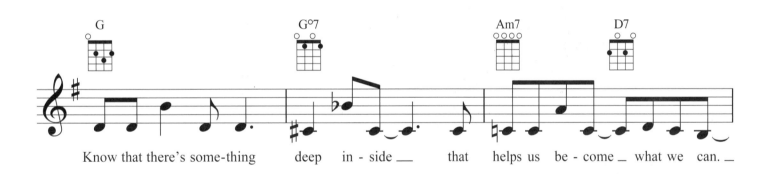

feel like this, ___ and know that the feel - ing is real - ly mine.

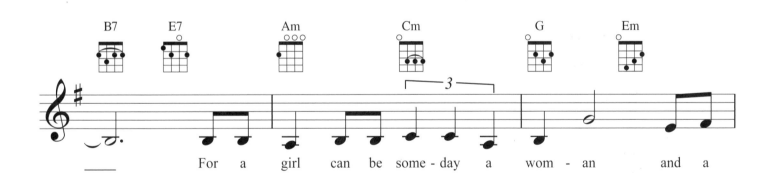

Know that there's some-thing deep in - side ___ that helps us be - come _ what we can. _

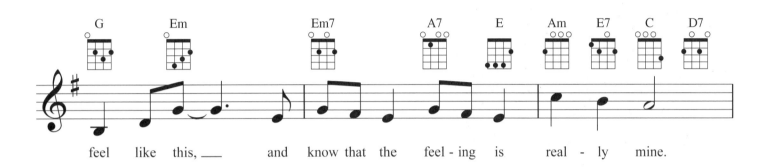

___ For a girl can be some - day a wom - an and a

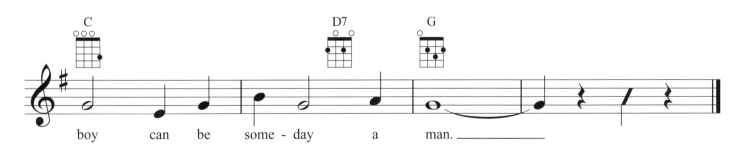

boy can be some - day a man. _____

Sometimes People Are Good

Words and Music by Fred Rogers

First note

Verse

Moderately

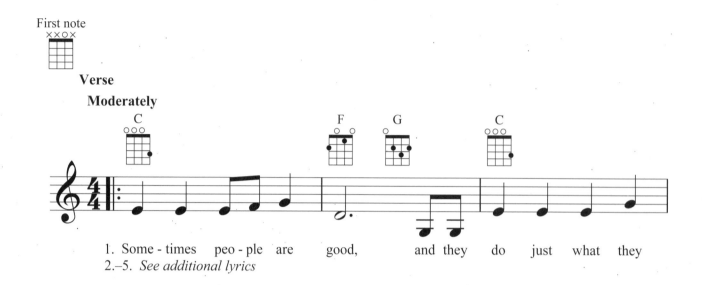

1. Some - times peo - ple are good, and they do just what they
2.–5. *See additional lyrics*

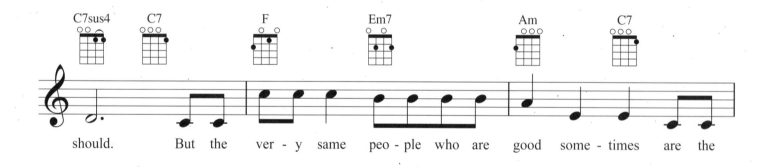

should. But the ver - y same peo - ple who are good some - times are the

ver - y same peo - ple who are bad some - times. It's fun - ny, but it's

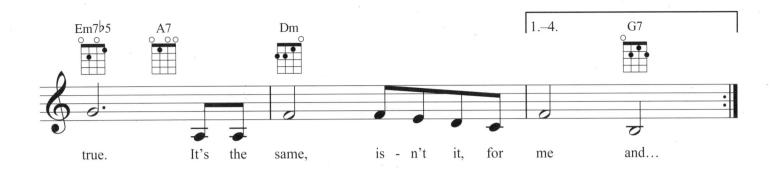

true.   It's   the   same,   is - n't it,   for   me   and…

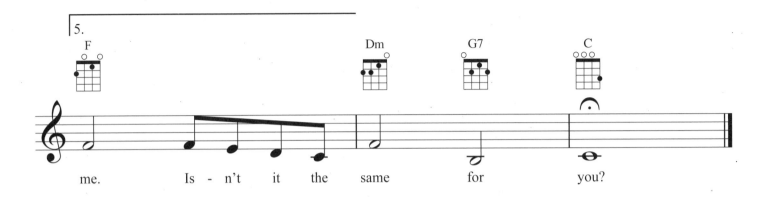

me.   Is - n't   it   the   same   for   you?

Additional Lyrics

2. Sometimes people get wet,
   And their parents get upset.
   But the very same people who are wet sometimes
   Are the very same people who are dry sometimes.
   It's funny, but it's true.
   It's the same, isn't it, for me and…

3. Sometimes people make noise,
   And they break each other's toys.
   But the very same people who are noisy sometimes
   Are the very same people who are quiet sometimes.
   It's funny, but it's true.
   It's the same, isn't it, for me and…

4. Sometimes people get mad,
   And they feel like being bad.
   But the very same people who are mad sometimes
   Are the very same people who are glad sometimes.
   It's funny, but it's true.
   It's the same, isn't it, for me and…

5. Sometimes people are good,
   And they do just what they should.
   But the very same people who are good sometimes
   Are the very same people who are bad sometimes.
   It's funny, but it's true.
   It's the same, isn't it, for me.
   Isn't it the same for you?

There Are Many Ways
(To Say I Love You)
Words and Music by Fred Rogers

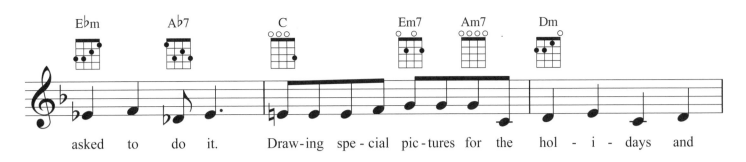

asked   to   do   it.   Draw-ing spe - cial pic-tures for the   hol - i - days   and

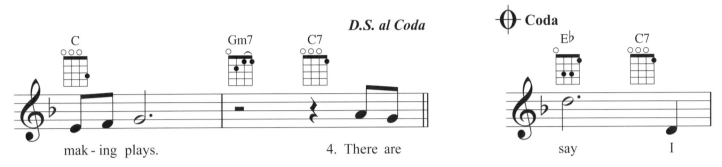

D.S. al Coda   **Coda**

mak - ing plays.   4. There are   say   I

Outro
Freely

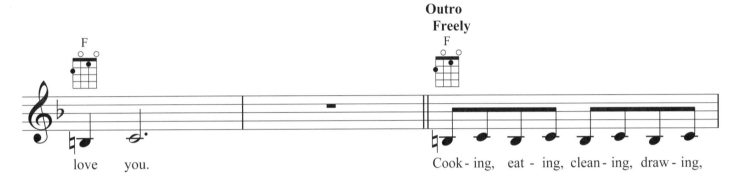

love   you.   Cook - ing, eat - ing, clean - ing, draw - ing,

play - ing, be - ing, un - der - stand - ing, love   you. _____

Additional Lyrics

2. There's the cooking way to say I love you.
   There's the cooking something someone really likes to eat.
   The cooking way, the cooking way,
   The cooking way to say I love you.

3. There's the eating way to say I love you.
   There's the eating something someone made especially.
   The eating way, the eating way,
   The eating way to say I love you.

4. There are many ways to say I love you.
   Just by being there when things are sad and scary.
   Just by being there, being there,
   Being there to say I love you.

When the Day Turns to Night

Words and Music by Fred Rogers

First note

Verse
Serenely, freely

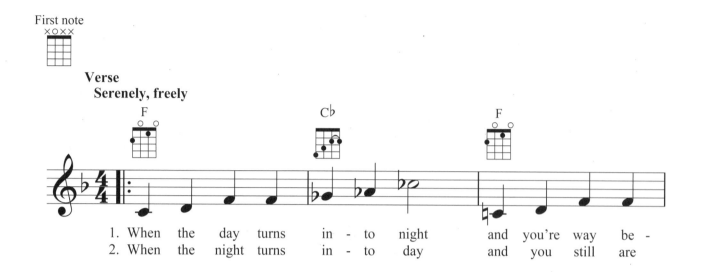

1. When the day turns in-to night and you're way be -
2. When the night turns in-to day and you still are

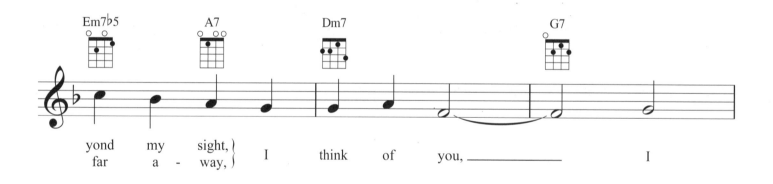

yond my sight,} I think of you, _____ I
far a - way,}

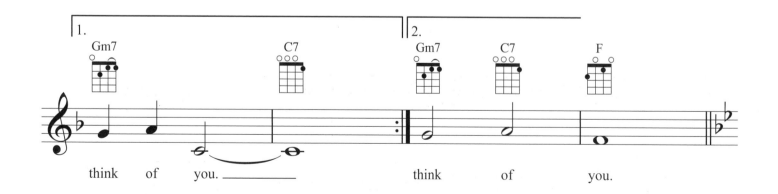

think of you. _____ think of you.

Bridge

E - ven when I am not here, we still can be so

ver - y near. I want you to know, my dear, I

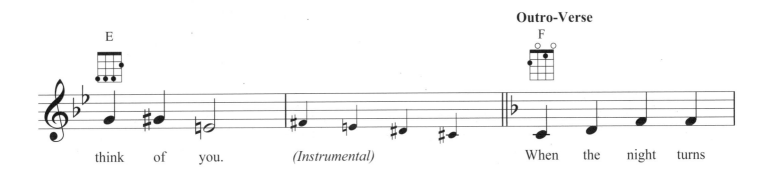

think of you. *(Instrumental)* **Outro-Verse** When the night turns

in - to day and you still are far a - way, I

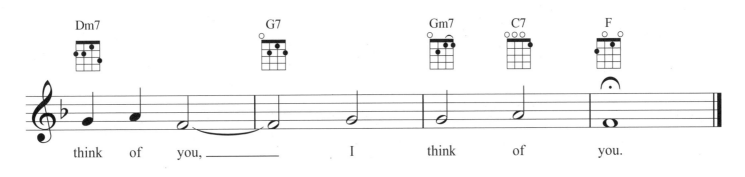

think of you, _____ I think of you.

Won't You Be My Neighbor?

(It's a Beautiful Day in the Neighborhood)

Words and Music by Fred Rogers

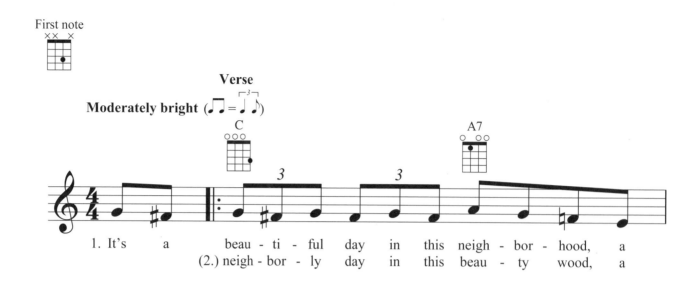

1. It's a beau-ti-ful day in this neigh-bor-hood, a
(2.) neigh-bor-ly day in this beau-ty wood, a

beau-ti-ful day for a neigh-bor. Would you be mine? _____ Could you
neigh-bor-ly day for a beau-ty. Would you be mine? _____ Could you

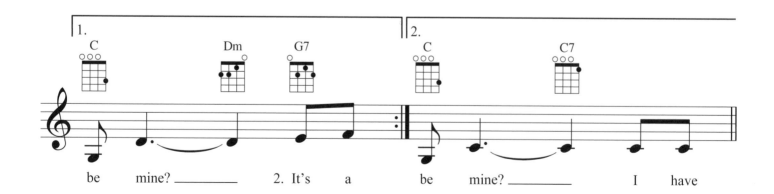

be mine? _____ 2. It's a   be mine? _____ I have

Bridge

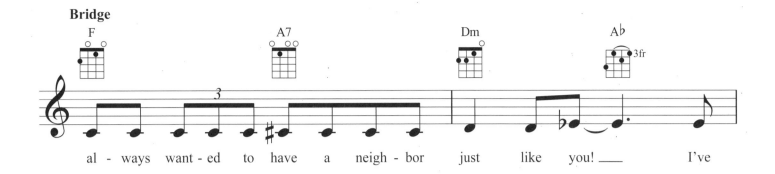

al - ways want - ed to have a neigh - bor just like you! ___ I've

al - ways want - ed to live in a neigh - bor - hood with you. ___ So,

Outro

let's make the most of this beau - ti - ful day. Since we're to - geth - er, we might as well say:

Would you be mine? Could you be mine? Won't you be my neigh - bor? ___

Won't you please, won't you please? Please won't you be my neigh - bor? ___

You Can Never Go Down the Drain

Words and Music by Fred Rogers

First note

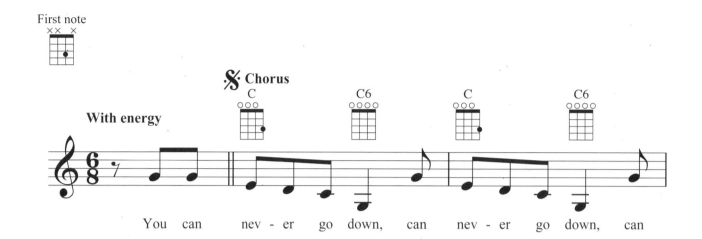

With energy

Chorus

You can nev-er go down, can nev-er go down, can

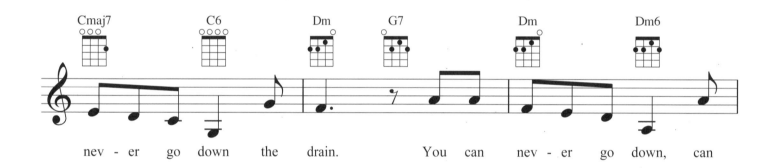

nev-er go down the drain. You can nev-er go down, can

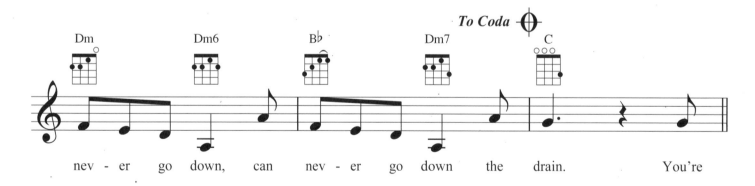

To Coda

nev-er go down, can nev-er go down the drain. You're

Bridge

big-ger than the wa-ter, _____ you're big-ger than the

soap, _____ you're much big - ger than all the bub - bles, _____ and

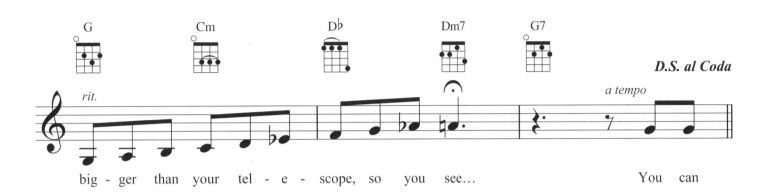

D.S. al Coda

big - ger than your tel - e - scope, so you see... You can

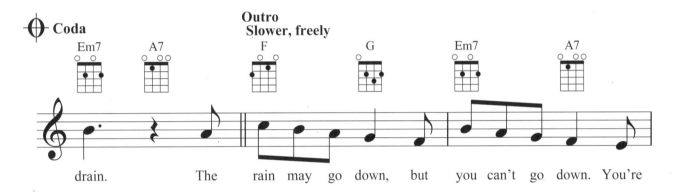

Coda   **Outro**
                  Slower, freely

drain.   The rain may go down, but you can't go down. You're

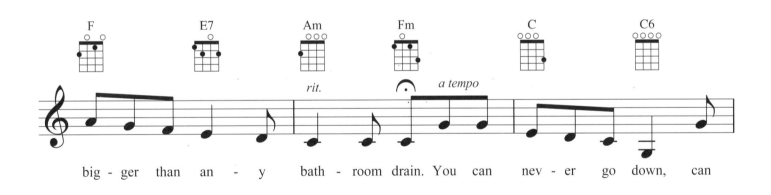

big - ger than an - y bath - room drain. You can nev - er go down, can

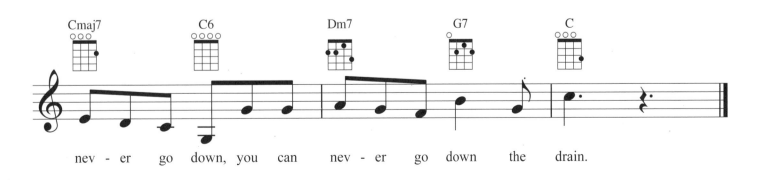

nev - er go down, you can nev - er go down the drain.

You're Growing

Words and Music by Fred Rogers

First note

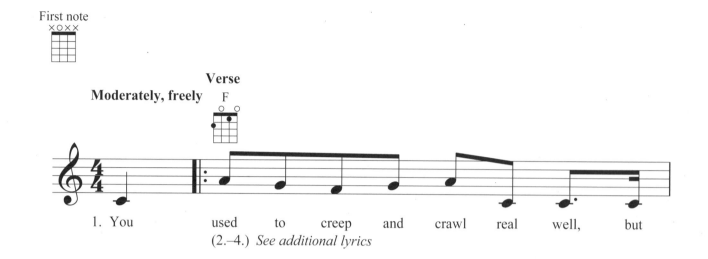

1. You used to creep and crawl real well, but
(2.–4.) *See additional lyrics*

then you learned to walk real well. There was a time you'd coo and cry, but

then you learned to talk and, my! You al - most al - ways try. You

al - most al - ways do your best. I like the way you're grow - ing up. It's

Chorus

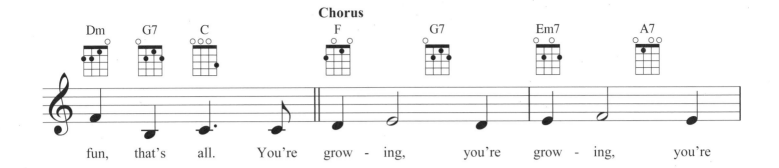

fun, that's all. You're grow - ing, you're grow - ing, you're

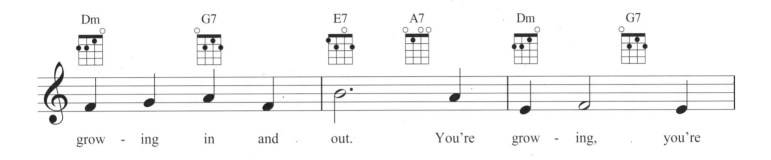

grow - ing in and out. You're grow - ing, you're

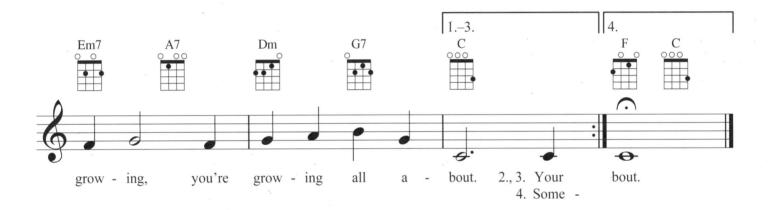

grow - ing, you're grow - ing all a - bout. 2., 3. Your bout.
4. Some -

Additional Lyrics

2. Your hands are getting bigger now.
   Your arms and legs are longer now.
   You even sense your insides grow
   When Mom and Dad refuse you, so
   You're learning how to wait now.
   It's great to hope and wait somehow.
   I like the way you're growing up.
   It's fun, that's all.

3. Your friends are getting better now.
   They're better every day somehow.
   You used to stay at home to play,
   But now you even play away.
   You do important things now,
   Your friends and you do big things now.
   I like the way you're growing up.
   It's fun, that's all.

4. Someday you'll be a grown-up too
   And have some children grow up too.
   Then you can love them in and out
   And tell them stories all about
   The times when you were their size;
   The times when you found great surprise
   In growing up. And they will sing,
   It's fun, that's all.

You've Got to Do It

Words and Music by Fred Rogers

First note

Verse

Freely

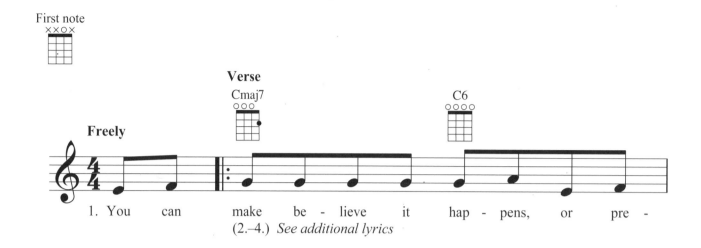

1. You can make be - lieve it hap - pens, or pre -
(2.–4.) *See additional lyrics*

tend that some-thing's true. You can wish or hope or con - tem - plate a

thing you'd like to do. But un - til you start to do it, you will

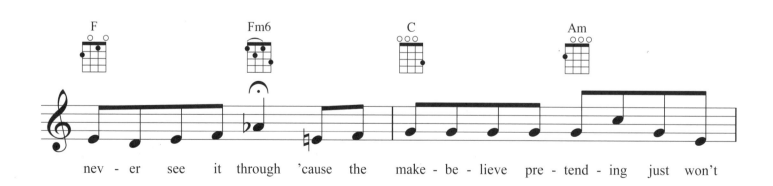

nev - er see it through 'cause the make - be - lieve pre - tend - ing just won't

Additional Lyrics

2. If you want to ride a bicycle
   And ride it straight and tall.
   You can't simply sit and look at it
   'Cause it won't move at all.
   But it's you who have to try it,
   And it's you who have to fall (sometimes)
   If you want to ride a bicycle
   And ride it straight and tall.

3. If you want to read a reading book
   And read the real words too,
   You can't simply sit and ask
   The words to read themselves to you.
   But you have to ask a person
   Who can show you one or two
   If you want to read a reading book
   And read the real words too.

4. It's not easy to keep trying,
   But it's one good way to grow.
   It's not easy to keep learning,
   But I know that this is so:
   When you've tried and learned
   You're bigger than you were a day ago.
   It's not easy to keep trying,
   But it's one good way to grow.

When a Baby Comes

Words and Music by Fred Rogers

Additional Lyrics

2. It can cry and it can holler,
   It can wet and make a face.
   But there's one thing it can never:
   It can never take your place.

3. You were there before the baby;
   Now the baby's always there.
   Now you wait for special moments
   With your mother in the chair.

4. You're a very special person,
   You are special to your mom.
   And your dad begins to say,
   "You'll always be the older one."

5. It's so good to know that always
   There's a special place for you,
   And a special place for baby
   Right inside the family, too.